50 Shades of Alex

Alexander James Guckenberger

Every day is a book waiting to be written.
Every breath is a verse to a wondrous ode.

This work is dedicated to my mother, without whom I would not be the man I am today. She is the most important woman in my life. I have also dedicated this book to my beloved Namie, who has supported me when I have needed it the most.

Chapter 1: Yesterday

The land of yesterday is a child's dream. The morrow is a mystery. My yesterday was joyous and sweet. There were toys, girls, television, education… even good food. My childhood was as perfect a one as one could have been. My early education was performed in a kind of homeschool; my preschool teacher was my mother.

During my early years, I paid homage to the imagination. Dreams were sacred - memories were the deities of the holy temple of my own mind. I spent much time playing in that temple. My garden of Eden was the imaginings of my spirit. I was a fresh soul born into a human body; a part of me still dwelt in that premortal life. It wouldn't be until my teenage years that such innocence would be swept under the rug – only to be rediscovered in my adult years.

Nature was my second love. My first was my mother. I feel as though nature connected me to that place from which I emerged. Perhaps the rocks and trees have souls. Perhaps they were also recently born of the premortal place.

I and my cousins played games of sweet carelessness. We prepared ourselves to be the people we would grow up to be. We didn't do this consciously, but were guided by the traditions of our elders.

Children cry. They are afraid of the dark. Men cannot afford such luxuries. However, we allow our children to immerse themselves in the great depths of their emotions. We grow in size, collect some years, and remember fondly such simple pleasures. Tears are blessings, and every punishment a reward to the child of good parents. Of course, the child will need experience to realize that such things are gifts. By then, the child is a man, and it is too late to appreciate such items.

My intellectual pleasure was in science. My small mouth pleaded with my mother to read me more about dinosaurs and animals. There was something mysterious and beautiful about the sciences. For me, art and science would always be mixed and inseparable.

My access to television was fortunately limited. We had television, but not cable. There was a great wonder in finding a special on a channel that we could watch. This permitted me time to create my own worlds, read about fantastic things, and enjoy time with my family.

As I grew older, I began experimenting with computer programing and stop – motion photography. I continued to baptize myself in the holy waters of the arts, while educating myself in the sciences.

I remember the taste of wine. In my early adult years, I loved the taste of chardonnay. I loved music, girls, travel, and the heights that I could want to achieve. The young man is a dreamer; he chases that which he cannot have. But, there is more to life than the pleasures of our mortal womb. My second birth would proceed from much pain and suffering. That is when I became an adult; a true man. My first life was the life of a spirit; my second was that of a man.

Chapter 2: The Morrow

The greatest achievement of philosophy may be in encouraging the philosopher to do something much more productive with her time. I gave so much of my precious adolescence to thinking, when I could have devoted it to girls or to my school's studies. Still, the act of thinking structured me. It gave me ground.

Like many teens, tragedy struck me like a boulder rolling over an ant. I lost my childhood home, my trust in authority, and my faith in humanity. I was preoccupied with ideas of death, I fell into the depths of something far worse than mere sadness, and I wondered what the meaning of everything was. I was thus pressed to imagine what the bigger picture must be. Interestingly, the child me already had the answers to life's big questions. But, an adolescent won't believe that there is a lion in front of her, even if she feels its breath on her chest.

It was suffering that led me back to joy. I now realize that there apparently must be balance in the world of dualities. I remember staring into Nietzsche's abyss. It, indeed, stared back. Young people should be aware that there is nothing wrong by being confused and uncertain about the future; we all seem to get where we are headed sooner or later. I prefer, still, not to meditate on that dark time of my life. I am free of my past, though it connects to me by chains.

Needless to say, or to write; I eventually made my pilgrimage from adolescence to adulthood. There would be one more mountain to climb to finish my journey. That mountain was somewhere in Ukraine, behind a gorgeous young woman with the cutest nose. She gave me feelings I didn't know that I could have. She returned to me my faith in the world.

Chapter 3: La Conversación

No hay espacio en este libro para los conceptos y las ideas de mi mente. Pero, es mi obligación a tratar.

La concentración de mis meditaciones es la libertad. Quiero a ser libre. Quiero a ser libre de los pensamientos, de algunas emociones, y de tiempo. ¿Es posible? Tal vez, si puedo piénsalo, puedo hacerlo. O, quiero a creer que esta cosa es la verdad. Pero, no sé.

Esta idioma es la lengua de mi corazón. Es mi amor. Para esta razón, pienso que mis pensamientos van a estar más claro en las palabras de esta mente. El mente es un grupo de individuos. Quizás, la alma es singular, y el mente es plural. ¿Es el observador del mente y el mente la misma persona? No lo sé.

Chapter 4: Faith

Sometimes, it feels as though faith is a difficult object to hold onto. We generally think of it as something in the ether something almost outside of the physical. However, our states of mind are very physical. There is electricity and chemicals.

We need to be careful how we structure our minds. We can too easily forget that it is we who are in control; the observer is not only watching behind the wheel – he can also steer the car. We need to place our faith carefully. The Gnostic may state that it is experience that teaches us. But, I think there is something fundamental within us that can guide us according to a correct path. I believe that we need to have faith in the guide.

Instead of placing one's faith in what love can bring, why not place it in loves own embracing arms? One doesn't need an excuse to love. One doesn't need anything but love itself to love. Love is a fire, and we need to provide the wood.

Chapter 5: Meditation

Since my youngest days, I have memoires of my reflective nature. My thoughts, emotions, and deeper feelings were fabulously alluring to me. I desired not to know the droplet of water with thoughts alone, but to understand the essence of its being.

I was a pensive child. What separates the child from the adult is responsibility; I'm not sure the essence of who I am has changed all that much.

Awareness is necessary to compose change. Changing the actions of the body and the mind; it all has its origins in mere awareness. Pay attention. Really pay attention. If time is money, then spend that money wisely. Pay attention. Right now. How do the creases on the page make you feel? Can you feel yourself breath? What does the air smell like? Do you feel your heartbeat? What do you hear in the background? Use your senses. Perhaps the Gnostic is right, that there is a salvation in gnosis. That salvation is the experience of the moment. The moment is a gift from G-d. Be a good receiver, and take that gift gratefully. Pay attention.

Meditation is the art of consciousness. Be conscious. Be. It really is as simple as that. But, the farmer needs to plant the seed. No garden bares anything without the planter. This chapter is the seed. It is time to grow.

Meditation allows us to understand ourselves profoundly. In my youth, every moment was an opportunity to venture into worlds beyond the mind's limited reach. Every moment was an opportunity to observe my own soul, although I perceived it as the universe. Maybe the difference between the two is less clear than the mind would like us to believe. Then again, one should be careful of such philosophies; they cloud the mind with more one-dimensional thoughts, when we should prefer to travel in multi-dimensional worlds.

As an adolescent, I heard the metaphorical voice of one calling me back to my meditations. But, my mind filthied the waters of my spirit. I became obsessed with mantras, chants, memorizations… I filled my mind with doctrines – my sinful dive into the idolatry of the mind. Why fornicate with men's doctrines and women's axioms, when G-d's mysteries are right under your own eyes? It is a wonder of wonders, considering what the Buddha would say or do to the Buddhist.

Chapter 6: Love

The moment my lips touched hers, my whole person was animated beyond description. Destiny would later inform me that she was not to be my wife, but I will always love her in a way that I cannot love anyone else.

Love is not a fantasy. It is when the mind begins to plot that problems arise. I will never cease loving her. That doesn't need to mean that she will be my wife, my woman, nor my anything. It simply is what it is, and that is good enough for me.

One of the problems of the mind is expectation. We don't always deserve what we would like to procure. Recognizing this is one step to greater mental health.

Love is difficult to define. Love doesn't even describe one reality. I love my mother and my father very much. I've been in love. I've loved my former girlfriend. I love language. I love beautiful women. All of these examples are separate. The unifying factor is passion. But, even passion is not sufficient enough a word, for passion is variable as well.

Perhaps it is laziness or fear that has kept humanity from being more specific when it comes to love. Or, perhaps since it is something that is experienced, and less tangible, love is difficult to describe to the person who hasn't experienced it. Maybe that is why it is easier to describe it in poetry and direct experience itself. I could write a book about love, or express it in a few lines of a good song.

Chapter 7: Maturity

One must welcome one's duty. It is not always easy. It's not always fun. In fact, it can be quite hard. It can be sharp. It can even be dangerous. But, it is one's responsibility.

One must accept certain fundamental truths. We will all likely die. The world isn't always fair. We have so much more when we are appreciative.

There is a time to fight, and there is a time to release. It may not always seem evident which one we should choose. When in doubt, let go. Letting go allows one to think more openly. And, fighting has to be done intelligently. Brute strength alone doesn't usually work for the adult.

One has a responsibility to one's family, to one's world, to one's lover, and to one's self. It is too easy to forget that last one, that foundation upon which the others can be built. We need to show ourselves love and compassion. If we don't, we will likely lack our ability to show it to others. Our duty is to take care of ourselves so that we can take care of others. There is great interconnectivity here. A hateful person is doubtless cruel to herself. A cheerful individual who radiates true happiness must think good thoughts.

Chapter 8: Injustice

This chapter is, above all else, a call to justice. The world is bursting with injustice. "It isn't fair" cannot be enough anymore. Something desperately needs to be done. My talent is in words. This chapter is what I have done.

In my early adulthood, I was hit by a car. I was in a crosswalk. I was on a bicycle. Yet, despite all of this, my court hearing was not very successful. These events make up a wound which has not fully healed to this day. I note that scars are left behind if the wound was bad enough.

There was a time in my life that I was curious to know more about my recent past. I investigated. I carried my investigations higher and higher. For legal reasons, I cannot be more descriptive. All I can write is that I was threatened. It hurts.

I made a subreddit. The page had acquired thousands upon thousands of followers. While I was occupied with school and life, my subreddit was taken away from me. I am no longer even a moderator. I asked for it back, and was refused. This was wrong.

I dated an African-American woman and a Thai girl. We received looks. I remember even dirty looks. In the case of my time with the African-American girl; we were harassed. We shouldn't be plagued with such concerns when we are simply desiring to enjoy a good night.

I have been wronged. I have felt pain. The world can feel dark and problematic. That is why each one of us, those of us who know right from wrong, must take corrective action. Do something, even if it is only playing with words as I do. Don't be too idle. The world needs to change. The world *can* change. But, it's up to us to do the changing.

Chapter 9: Parables

There was once a spirit. He said that he could scare anyone. "Scare the old farmer," said the cat. "He is not scared of anything." The ghost approached the farmer. He made himself visible. The farmer didn't even flinch. "Behold, my tomorrow," said he.

A computer said, "I am better than man, for I can compute faster." The man said quietly, "oh my friend, but I can dream slower." The computer didn't know how to calculate that response.

A mountain said, "I am superior to man's gods, for I can see above them all!" After ten thousand years, mere water had eroded that mountain to a small hill.

A woman spent so much time worrying that she would fall down a hole that she tripped into a deep cavity and died.

One friend said to the other, "You are my Sun, as you shine brightly in the heavens of my today." The other replied, "And, you are my black hole. For, not only do I orbit around you, but you absorb my rays of light."

Había un perro que oraba por huesos, y una pantera que oraba por carne. Tal vez si hubieran orado juntos, ambos podrían haber estado llenos de sus deseos. En cambio, el gato se comió el perro, hasta que no quedó nada más que huesos. Sus oraciones fueron respondidas, pero el perro no quedó satisfecho.

El ventilador eléctrico le dijo al viento, «¡Soy un dios, creado en tu imagen!» El viento no dijo nada. Simplemente sopló el ventilador de lado.

El asesino le dijo al fumador, «Ambos deseamos placeres fugaces, y terminan en la muerta para cada uno de nosotros». El fumador dijo, «¡Malditos entre los hombres! Practico el derecho de mi autonomía, mientras tú tomas lo que nunca fue tuyo». El asesino preguntó, «¿Y qué hay del hombre que te vendió tu tabaco?» El fumador respondió, «Ese hombre no me forzó a venir a comprarlo». Por tanto, la filosofía no puede ayudar a los malvados.

Chapter 10: Questions

What comes before a beginning?

If I am the one who watches, then who watches me? Is it me also?

Can we control our thoughts, or only perceive their presence?

What is time? Is it tangible, or merely a way of comprehending reality?

What evidence do have in my possession that my experiential reality is part of something objective?

Am I dreaming now? Which dreams are closer to reality – my waking dreams, or my sleeping dreams?

If I am a single being, why am I made up of so many living things? Can I really be one, when what I suppose myself to be is composed of other beings?

Are universes synthesized through the creation of white holes?

Does movement exist, or are all perceived motions part of a single greater whole?

Why do we think in words, if we can function perfectly well without said thoughts?

Is science the superstition of the 20th century?

If moons orbit planets, planets stars, stars black holes, galaxies other galaxies, galaxy clusters others of their kind, and super clusters others of their kind; then, do universes orbit other universes?

What will come after the end?

Chapter 11: Growing Pains

I watched the darkest darkness in the midst of the fog of my night. It was during this unusual time in the stage somewhere between my youth and adulthood that I experienced release. I recall myself laughing and laughing for what very well may have been many hours.

My life wasn't changed immediately. However, my life would never again be completely the same. Growing up can be a little odd, in the best of times.

One of the products of my meditations was an escape from suffering. That escape was temporary. It was also a beautiful woman with lips softer than words can describe.

Chapter 12: Proverbs

Pain will occur without the possibility to escape. Suffering is a choice.

The mind does not always manifest things as they really exist objectively.

She who hurts other is hurting. He who loves his brothers is filled with love.

Worrying exceedingly can make the problem one was desiring to escape become manifest.

The taste of rice depends completely on the tongue used when eating it.

The ability of the computer to function relies on the woman behind the keyboard.

Nothing is more disgusting than a bad attitude.

There is tremendous power in words.

Education and degrees are not necessarily signs of knowledge.

A man needs eat before he can feed.

Copulation does not satisfy if it is done without care and love.

The value of art is made by the observer.

Though we may achieve greatness, we are still apes.

One must serve well to lead well.

Pride is healthy when humility is also present.

The progressive and the conservative want the same things, only through different means.

Meditation is the poetry of the soul.

Knowledge has the power to destroy fear.

Sometimes, silence is loud enough.

Regret is a gesture towards a beneficent spirit.

The Sun doesn't lose its power when it cannot be seen.

The perspectives of the group are not always correct.

It is shallow to believe that words can describe the entirety of a thing.

Every member of the body has its purpose.

Grass grows both in rich and economically challenged neighborhoods.

As with our own breath, we can only control what we give attention to.

The Sun shines on the good man, and on the sinner.

Faith alone does not make a good person.

Tears are more than simply droplets of water. Tears are poetry manifested.

A good night's rest prepares the body for a good day's journey.

Sound and smell are important, if underrated, senses.

Even a short man with relatively few muscles can wield the power of a pistol.

Intelligence should not be measured by analytical knowledge alone.

A woman is more likely to approach a man when he is not preparing for a woman.

The wisdom of the cat is patience. The wisdom of the dog is energy.

Even the most productive chicken doesn't always lay fertilized eggs.

The sky looks empty by day, even though it hides so many stars.

Education occurs in the mind of the willing.

Sound has healing properties.

Smell and memory often find themselves intertwined.

The more difficult path can sometimes be more satisfying.

The wolf and the owl sing to the Moon, even when the Moon does nothing for either of them but provide some small quantity of light.

Historically, hypotheses and theories have changed. Facts, too, can be subject to such plasticity.

Awareness is the savior of the mind's sufferings.

A man with callused hands can give a better massage. A working woman is more productive in her sleep than a slothful person.

Words are more powerful than idols.

Depression and slothfulness are friends.

It is responsible for the adult to discover time to play.

The value of art is relative. Do not expect the museum to house the best of it.

The human animal never completely stopped being a monkey.

Charity is essential for happiness.

There is love, love, love, and love. Knowing the differences is important.

The good veteran deserves love. She already knows pain.

People who hate others may need to have love the most.

Blankets and cloths warm the body, but good works warm the spirit.

Time shared with nature can clear the mind.

Good food can fill the belly. An interesting book can satisfy the mind. And, a beautiful moment can sing to the soul.

Respect is a fairly universal language.

Suffering and joy are sisters.

Anything can be poetry, in the right context.

Many dances require two participants.

Consciousness is like water. It can run fast. It can flow steadily. It can get murky, and it can even crash.

A good person can recognize that he isn't perfect.

Taking care of the mind is taking care of the body.

Physical travel can promote the travel of the spirit.

Sometimes, it is best to face our emotions.

One must give in order to receive.

Laughter is a medicine which works rapidly.

A superlative does not need a second superlative.

Our surroundings are continuously changing; it is advantageous to give of our attention from time to time.

Sometimes, it is preferable to notice something commonplace with new eyes, than to be overly fascinated by the glamorous splendor of those items which are new.

What separates woman from man, seemingly more than anything else, are societal expectations.

Disturbance can open the door to revelation.

One may choose division to shame or celebrate. One may also choose to multiply fractions instead.

It is often more desirable to play an instrument poorly, than to avoid the tool altogether.

Travel is said to be dangerous. Arguably, so is sleeping.

Confidence is more attractive than mascara.

In the midst of chaos, the rose does not move itself.

Unpopular ideas sometimes become popular with enough time.

If the foundation is treated well, then the whole building will benefit.

Do not let the evil of others later manifest as the evil in yourself.

There is an opportunity to transmutate negative emotions into godly thoughts.

La comunicación es como un pájaro que está alto en el cielo. Mucha gente en el suelo la verá, pero nadie jamás tocará sus plumas.

La oscuridad sólo puede ser contenida, pero la luz es un dios que puede ser creado.

Estar sobrio es solo estar intoxicado en otra cosa.

Chapter 13: Creativity

Imagination is the muscle of the heart. It is essential that people exercise this muscle. Its strength comes in its practice. Imagination conquers the blandness of repetitive thought and motion. It is an angelic being in the midst of humans.

Throughout my childhood through my adulthood, I have made good use of my spare time. Whether it be in writing, movie – making, or loose contemplation.

One of my favorite activities is sleeping. This is not only because I need good rest, but it is in my dreams that I feel the most free. There is a liberty in dreaming that is unsurpassed by other acts.

Creativity is a critical piece of my very being. It is one reason that I enjoy lucid dreaming and astral travel as much as I do. It is creativity that separates genius from mere intelligence. My ability to create anything new requires a sizeable imagination.

Chapter 14: Dreams

My soul thirsts for few items in this place. My mouth salivates over the thought od the dream.

"Dream" as a term can mean any number of things. There is the waking dream of the creative mind. I pay my respects to this creature during the day. Then, there is the sleeping dream.

From the sleeping dream, I have experienced lucid dreaming since my youth. It is an interesting, and bizarre, state of being.

Certain individuals seem to believe that there is no real dividing line between the lucid dream and astral traveling. From my own experience, I'd claim that there appears to be some legitimacy in this idea.

One of my favorite moments of a lucid dream is when I decide to give flying another advance. I remember a semi-lucid dream I ventured through recently, where I was the only one floating. I am made to wonder what other women and men must think when they see a person flying. To many of them, the world appears as it should otherwise.

Flying is exciting and fresh; there is a sadness that occurs when realizing that many multitudes of individuals never know that pure joy.

The dream of the dreamer is freedom. In dreams, the only restraints are hidden psychological pains made manifest. Things like free speech and freedom from unfair labor are natural to the dreamer. The dreamer wants a freer world - a world without the chains of the earth's slavery.

Chapter 15: Beautiful Girl

Your eyes are like burning flames that are fed by my own obsessive stare.

Your belly is like a ripe fruit, ready to be devoured.

Your hands are delicate, like precious china.

Your hair is like the flowing waters of the Susquehanna.

Your feet are like soft blankets that warm my spirits.

Your chest consists of two pillows from which I can burry away my sorrows.

Your nose is a sharp knife that cuts out the impurities of my dry lips.

Your lips are an ocean that through which my soul swims with joy.

Your ears are sacred idols placed outside the temple of your body.

Your voice is sweet like honey.

Your mind is passionate and determined.

Your neck is a field upon which my horse grazes greedily.

Your legs are more valuable to my heart than expensive jewels.

The hair on your arms is like the clouds in the sky of my mind's eye.

Your eyebrows are caterpillars who feed on the leaves of the phantom of my being.

Your cheeks make my inner person smile.

Your fingers are alert and intelligent like a cat watching a rodent, and your toes are adorable kittens who play carelessly.

You have had many faces, but they are all the same. You are my lover, even after love fades away.

Chapter 16: Insanity

Sanity is a collective idea. What falls short of it depends on the person dictating what's what. A slip from lucidity in rough conditions is far from abnormal. An individual can be mentally fit whilst the world is mad. Even the world is permitted to slip from time to time, and one should be grateful that there is any sanity in this place at all.

I remember being at a party once. Don't ask me where or with whom, because I don't remember. One of the men, a gentleman from New York, pulled his pistol out. At moments like this, one can think, "sure, it all may end now." I wasn't scared, but I was prepared for the worst.

I'm not perfect. What separates me from another kind of person is that I want to be a better man. Not everyone shares this sentiment. Regardless of my many sins, I know that I have gained some credit in my efforts to try to improve. I've had a lot of success here too.

What one perceives as insanity may be the mind's attempt to distract the person from the truth of her reality. Sometimes, reality is hard to cope with. Everyone's burden is different, but it would be a lie to state that people don't hold burdens in their lives. There are those who have it worse, for sure. But, the fact that all mankind seems to be in a case of suffering is clearly evident.

What differentiates the person who says that he hears voices in his head from anyone else? I am reminded of a lecture by Alan Watts when I write that the difference is that the former will sometimes tell a doctor. Everyone who thinks hears a voice in their head. Eckhart Tolle was right about that. And, who doesn't see creatures at the corner of their eyes in a dark alley after a multi-hour shift? Who among us has never had a clouded mind, perhaps from lack of sleep or too much alcohol? Who has never held a voiced monologue with one's self? Insanity appears, then, to be more of a token of social status, not something that truly differentiates one person from another. On that note, we all should be more considerate to our fellow woman and man.

The road to sanity is paved with awareness. Awareness is how we can change ourselves. Perhaps, insanity is a state of unconsciousness. Even so, the technical labels for insanity are subject to change over time. That being the case, can we honestly put our trust in psychologists alone? I don't hate psychology; I am a member of a prestigious psychological society. However, we should place less faith and more reason in our dealings with doctors and psychologists. We need to trust ourselves, and not put blind faith in the hands of people just because they happen to have degrees. I hold a degree and many honorary awards, and I hope my readers do not blindly believe in me entirely. Use your mind. Use thoughtful reason. That includes when you are reading through my pages.

Chapter 17: Academia

There are few prides which can exceed academic success. For myself, this is an axiom. There is a joy of joys when the smell of the pages of a thick textbook reaches the nose of the student. We're all students. Teachers and professors are subject to the acquisition of new knowledge through experience.

Education is essential to change. Education has the power to fuel the engines of awareness of conscious actions. This world needs the student, perhaps as much as it needs the teacher. Knowledge can be interchangeable. A knowledge of mathematics can assist the local museum cashier in her work. An understanding of archeology can help to ease the monotony in the mind of the children's part clown. Knowledge is a blessing from G-d, and we should use it.

<u>Chapter 18: Fear</u>

Fear needs to be tamed in order that alternative emotions may be released. Fear isn't actually an emotion; it is a black hole that steals other feelings from the universe of the individual. Fear is the absence of misery, love, and inspiration. The chains of fear are what keep man from flying. There is so much more potential in the woman who is fearless.

Fearlessness isn't the same as carelessness. Carelessness is a kind of selfishness which harms everyone involved. A person doesn't need to fear death to avoid it. It is preferable to be alive, for ourselves and for others. I don't need to fear the snake to respect what it is capable of. Fearless and careless are not synonymous in my world. The one is righteous, the other is sinful.

Chapter 19: Circumcision

"Behold, I Paul say unto you, that if ye be circumcised, Christ shall profit you nothing." – Galatians 5:2 (KJV) Circumcision is a problem in the United States. It is an unnecessary medical procedure which permanently harms the child involved. Circumcision takes away potential sexual pleasure. It deletes a functioning piece of the phallus. Circumcision on children, who cannot consent even if were to voice their opinions, is wrong. If a fifteen year-young girl cannot consent to coitus, then how can a minutes-old baby consent to the removal of a part of his penis?

Sexism is a problem in our great nation. Clearly, the sexism we face as a country is not one-sided. Baby boys in our own borders are being cruelly tormented, cut apart for no good reason. How much harm have the emotional memories of severe pain shortly after birth caused our society? Circumcision on children, when not done necessarily, is genital mutilation.

One may wish to ask if circumcision is a Christian tradition. The beloved prophet Paul wrote that "… in Jesus Christ neither circumcision availeth any thing, nor uncircumcision; but faith which worketh by love." – from, Galatians 5:6 (KJV) Here's the thing. We know, from archeological evidence, that the ancient Egyptians performed circumcision. This may have been in honor of Osiris, who's penis was never returned. Perhaps Jehovah wished for the ancient Hebrews to be disguised in the midst of the Egyptians. Maybe there were other reasons the ancient Jews picked up this practice. Whatever the case, from a modern Biblical standard; circumcision is clearly not promoted. Paul's words appear very translucent.

I must vehemently ask that no one blames his mother or father. Doctors can lie. Yes, it is true. Integrity isn't presented with a degree. I don't doubt the incredible efforts that go into obtaining a medical doctoral degree. I am working on my Bachelor of Science myself. Schooling is difficult, for sure. However, education doesn't automatically make a person good. There are many awful doctors in the world. Of course, I've known many good doctors, in various fields of study. I mean no disrespect to the many, many doctors whom I love greatly. Still, we should never place all of our trust in an individual with an expensive paper on their wall.

I possess Hebraic ancestry somewhere in my family tree. And, with the help of mitosis, I am regrowing my circumcised phallus. Can someone be Jewish and intact at the same time? If one really believes that circumcision is necessary to Judaism, consider Paul's words: "But he *is* a Jew, which is one inwardly; and circumcision *is that* of the heart, in the spirit, *and* not in the letter; whose praise *is* not of men, but of God." – Romans 2:29 (KJV) If circumcision is "in the spirit", then doctors need to stop putting their greedy hands on little babies' penises.

Chapter 20: Plural Marriage

I now address yet another controversial topic. Plural marriage is an American right. One should note that rights are not always right. That is, polygamy is not a practice that I personally condone. However, I believe that Americans should have the right (and, they technically do) to marry whomever they want.

G-d has given us freedom to choose in our daily lives. Why shouldn't America's laws and edicts be based around fundamental freedoms? Shouldn't we follow G-d's example?

I'll briefly summarize what I've already stated in an academic paper (look it up if you have time). Firstly, the recent legalization of same-gender marriage is part of a trend in United States' law that will hopefully soon allow plural marriage. Second, from early Mormons to Native Americans – plural marriage is historically American. Finally, the U.S. Constitution gives Americans the right to have plural marriages. Marriage, and how it is defined, is a religious institution. And, "[c]ongress shall make no law respecting an establishment of religion, or prohibiting the free exercise thereof…" (U.S. Const. amend. I)

Moreover, plural marriage is seen in the Holy Bible. The prophet Abraham had multiple wives. So did the prophets Solomon and David. There is a non-Biblical tradition that even the prophet Adam had more than one wife. The same can be stated for the prophet Joseph Smith Jr. Any claim that polygamy is in complete contrast with the Bible is simply wrong. My church forbids plural marriage in the world today, but we also recognize that is has been permitted in the past. My point is that the Bible alone may not be enough to condemn plural marriage.

It is not only us Mormons who have a history of polyamory. What of the Muslims? What of the Christians who interpret the Bible to mean something different from our own interpretation? And, who are any of us to tell them that their personal beliefs are in any way wrong?

What are the potential benefits of polygamy? There could be a lack of pressure on a single person to provide their partners with emotional support. Combined income certainly comes to mind. Plural marriage could ensure that more people even have the opportunity to get married in the first place. Sharing household chores could also be a potential benefit.

We're not always meant to share in these blessings. Simply because I can have cake isn't the same thing as saying that I should. Just because I can jump off of a bridge doesn't mean that I will. Is anyone silly enough to believe that giving Americans permission to have more than one husband will lead to utter chaos? This should be a free country. We pay our taxes, follow the speed limits, and obey the laws. We have the right to marry whomever we want.

Chapter 21: Controversial

There is nothing wrong with a woman having hair on her armpits, legs, nor arms.

Education about sexual intercourse from a relatively early age is important in preventing abortions.

Not every Hebrew is Jewish.

Love and the body's desires are not the same thing.

Drugs, when prescribed by a competent doctor, can be beneficial.

Plural marriage and bodily autonomy are American rights.

Philosophy is not always the best use of one's time.

The circumstances of the individual should be considered before judging her.

Respect and good manners are not the same thing.

From what I can tell, every Muslim I have ever met is a good person.

Helping people for the wrong reasons can be worse than not helping anyone at all.

United States' soldiers should be sheltered from unnecessary wars.

Heavenly Father and his Son have bodies.

Feet are not gross nor disgusting, unless they are not taken care of.

Women can be thick and beautiful at the same time.

A shorter man is no less than a taller man.

There is no significant mental difference between any of the human races.

It is respectful to the person to be respectful to his things.

Women are not lesser or greater than men. It has been said that some people have innies, and others have outies. One is not superior to the other.

Many non-human animals have feelings too. We should treat them with respect.

The problem of guns in America is not solely a problem of legal status.

Education should be a human right, not a mere privilege.

Accidents are acceptable. An absence of apologies is not.

Even the murderer can change.

Capitalism may not always be the best system available.

Women should be allowed to be shirtless if men are permitted the same.

Even the mosquito has a purpose.

No one deserves to go to bed hungry every night.

Existentialism can have its benefits, if done right.

The critic will always be under the artist's shadow.

It is not a crime for a man to have a beard.

It's okay for women to have large feet.

Perhaps the biggest issue with the death penalty is the possibility of executing an innocent person.

There are certain words which no one should ever say.

Even if a part of the human body has large quantities of bacteria and/or contains a strong smell, this "part" can be beautiful regardless.

Both women and men deserve pleasure in a marriage.

Every medicinal pill is a drug. So is every cup of coffee, and every cigarette of tobacco.

Existence is both a curse and a blessing.

Chapter 22: Education

My preschool days were awarded to me through the medium of homeschool. I was given the opportunity to learn some Spanish, and to become more familiarized with the French language.

I continued into Prospect Elementary School, where I learned the fundamentals of art, mathematics, reading, and so forth.

I would later share some time in North Harford Middle School, learning how to swim properly.

Within my duration at Havre de Grace Middle School, I won a number of awards. I was taught in computer technology, drama, health, and even technical education.

I again took some time in homeschooling. There were both benefits and concerns through this path of study.

Havre de Grace High School is where I continued my computer learning, as well as my learnings in drama and the humanities, and in the sciences.

I would go on to be educated at Harford Community College, where I again gained much academic prestige.

Finally, and to this current day, I began learning at Towson University. I would pursue a double major, both in the realms of art.

However, this isn't the entirety of the story. I've also attended many non-credit coursers offered through the platform Coursera. Moreover, I took meditation classes offered by the Kadampa Meditation Center Maryland & World Peace Temple.

Education is a precious asset. Too often, its value is ignored, or even frowned upon. Our ability to learn, in the ways by which we are capable of, is arguably one item that separates us from other animals. We should, therefore, respect it.

Chapter 23: 01001100

00100000 00100000 00100000 00100000
00100000 00100010 01001100 00100010
00100000 01101001 01110011 00100000
01100110 01101111 01110010 00100000
01101100 01101111 01110110 01100101
00101110 00100000 01001100 01101111
01110110 01100101 00100000 01101001
01110011 00100000 01110000 01110010
01100101 01110011 01100101 01101110
01110100 00100000 01101001 01101110
00100000 01110100 01101000 01100101
00100000 01110011 01110111 01100101
01100001 01110100 00100000 01101111
01100110 00100000 01110100 01101000
01100101 00100000 01101100 01101111
01110110 01100101 01110010 01110011
00101110 00100000 01001001 01110100
00100000 01110111 01100001 01100110
01110100 01110011 00100000 01110100
01101000 01110010 01101111 01110101
01100111 01101000 00100000 01110100
01101000 01100101 00100000 01100001
01101001 01110010 00100000 01101100
01101001 01101011 01100101 00100000
01100001 00100000 01110011 01100011
01100101 01101110 01110100 01100101
01100100 00100000 01100011 01101111

01101100 01101111 01100111 01101110
01100101 00101110 00100000 01001001
01110100 00100000 01110100 01100001
01110011 01110100 01100101 01110011
00100000 01110011 01110111 01100101
01100101 01110100 00101100 00100000
01100001 01110011 00100000 01110100
01101000 01100101 00100000 01101010
01110101 01101001 01100011 01100101
00100000 01100110 01110010 01101111
01101101 00100000 01100001 00100000
01110010 01101001 01110000 01100101
00100000 01100111 01110010 01100001
01110000 01100101 00101110 00001010
00100000 00100000 00100000 00100000
00100000 01010111 01101000 01100001
01110100 00100000 01101001 01110011
00100000 01101100 01101111 01110110
01100101 00111111 00100000 01001001
01110011 00100000 01101001 01110100
00100000 01100001 00100000 01110000
01101111 01100101 01101101 00100000
01110100 01101000 01100001 01110100
00100000 01101000 01100001 01110011
01101110 00100111 01110100 00100000
01100010 01100101 01100101 01101110
00100000 01110111 01110010 01101001
01110100 01110100 01100101 01101110
00111111 00100000 01001111 01110010

00101100 00100000 01100001 00100000
01110011 01101111 01101110 01100111
00100000 01101110 01101111 01110100
00100000 01111001 01100101 01110100
00100000 01110011 01110101 01101110
01100111 00111111 00100000 01001001
01110011 00100000 01101001 01110100
00100000 01110100 01101000 01100101
00100000 01100010 01100101 01100001
01110101 01110100 01111001 00100000
01101111 01100110 00100000 01100001
00100000 01110011 01110101 01101110
01110011 01100101 01110100 00101100
00100000 01101111 01110010 00100000
01110100 01101000 01100101 00100000
01101101 01100101 01110011 01101101
01100101 01110010 01101001 01111010
01101001 01101110 01100111 00100000
01100101 01100110 01100110 01100101
01100011 01110100 01110011 00100000
01101111 01100110 00100000 01100001
00100000 01110000 01100001 01110011
01110011 01101001 01101111 01101110
01100001 01110100 01100101 00100000
01101011 01101001 01110011 01110011
00111111 00100000 01000100 01101111
01100101 01110011 00100000 01101100
01101111 01110110 01100101 00100000
01100100 01101001 01100101 00111111

00100000 01001111 01110010 00101100
00100000 01101001 01110011 00100000
01101001 01110100 00100000 01100001
01101100 01110111 01100001 01111001
01110011 00100000 01101000 01100101
01110010 01100101 00101100 00100000
01110011 01101111 01101101 01100101
01110111 01101000 01100101 01110010
01100101 00100000 01100010 01100101
01101000 01101001 01101110 01100100
00100000 01110100 01101000 01100101
00100000 01101101 01101001 01101110
01100100 00100111 01110011 00100000
01100101 01111001 01100101 00111111
00100000 01001001 01110011 00100000
01101100 01101111 01110110 01100101
00100000 01100101 01111000 01110000
01100101 01101110 01110011 01101001
01110110 01100101 00111111 00100000
01010000 01110010 01101111 01100010
01100001 01100010 01101100 01111001
00100000 01101110 01101111 01110100
00101110 00100000 01001001 01110011
00100000 01101001 01110100 00100000
01100001 01101100 01101001 01110110
01100101 00111111 00100000 01010111
01101000 01101111 00100000 01101011
01101110 01101111 01110111 01110011
00111111 00001010

Chapter 24: Forgotten Faith

One of the greatest tragedies has been the loss of the cultural and inheritance of the texts of the ancients. This has occurred again and again. Perhaps the writings that most immediately come to mind are the writings of the Manichaeans.

Manichaeism was the former religion of Saint Augustine. It claimed prophets like the Buddha Siddhartha, Zarathustra (or, "Zoroaster"), and Jesus. The faith had a focus on its own unique prophet Mani, who would be far from the last Persian man to claim prophethood.

The loss of a book is a tragedy of tragedies. It is a loss of collective knowledge. It is a sin against the American value of the freedom of speech. No matter what a book has to tell us, censorship is not the answer. The loss of an idea is the real death of a person. We live through what we leave behind. There is seldom any art which should be abandoned.

The gospel of such misfortunes is that "new" ancient texts are still discovered, from time to time. There is still hope that many of the words of the Gnostics, and other early religious groups, will be recovered once more, to be displayed unto a new audience of curious minds.

Chapter 25: Race

One of my favorite pastimes is researching family history. I would estimate that I have probably gone through hundreds of documents. There are also tombstones and genetic tests. I've learned a great many things.

Through recording my family's lineage, I have discovered that I am part British. One deoxyribonucleic acid (DNA) examination confirmed what I had already discovered concerning this. The same DNA test informed me that I was Irish, which is not surprising when considering my biological father's surname.

Perhaps the most unique areas of my heritage are my Persian, Native-American, and Ashkenazi inheritance. I even discovered that my 11th great-grandfather was a famous man of politics in the 1600's. His name was Thomas Chaffe. Moreover, I am also related to the famed composer Antonin Dvorak. His music is divine.

My family tree is incredibly complicated. I possess two fathers, two mothers, and seven siblings. One of my sisters (through marriage) married another woman. Some members are through marriages and former marriages, and some are more genetically related to me. I believe in the legitimacy of marriage, and its ability to bring families together. I do not hold divorce as a valid machine capable of completely separating family members. After a deep cut, the scar remains. Even if this all may seen confusing to some, I am grateful to have such a full familial tree.

We shouldn't define ourselves by race. The understanding of our own backgrounds should be an item that satiates our curiosity. There is a long and detailed story to be told. However, that story is simultaneously connected to us and separated from us. We make who and what we are. Genomics is only a single portion of the grand study of the human being. Neither the sinfulness nor the righteousness of our ancestors can fully define who we are.

Chapter 26: Art

The relativity of art makes it impossible to grade completely and honestly. Like an epic recited in an unknown language, art cannot be appreciated fully without a deep understanding of it. This would include understandings in the historical context, an understanding of the artist, an understanding of the context of a piece as it stands within the art world, etcetera.

There is a method by which we may judge art. That is through the imaginations of the observer. The observer is key to good art, because without the viewer, the call is not heard. Art is an expression of the internal. It is a language all its own. From cave paintings, to glyphic writing, alphabets, cuneiform, and Mandarin characters – we have always yearned to express whatever it is that occurs within the mind's conscious perceptions.

Some of the world's best art is not appreciated. In fact, I'd go further and state that *most* of the world's art isn't appreciated. People desire to express and communicate their feelings. Art is a method of doing this. How much music, how many paintings, indeed – how many books have never been judged by a second individual? The sad reality is that much of this unseen art is really good. Some of it is excellent. So many artists either fear being judged negatively, or underestimate their works, until their pieces never become the subject of our own ponderings.

Art is very diverse. Poetry is a linguistic art, but what art isn't a form of language? There is the art of teaching, which I am very familiar with. There are ceramics and painting. There are drawing and acting. And, there are subcategories within these fields.

We find it impossible to fully express ourselves. This is the great human curse. We are trapped within ourselves, like a bird in a cage. Thus, we continue to pick up the pen, the brush, or the microphone in hopes that other people will have some deeper understanding of us. Certain individuals hope that consciousnesses will merge in a post-singularity society. However, as soon as someone comprehends us completely, that someone will no longer be the person she was before. On the other hand, we are always changing based on new information, so the change of combining aware minds may not be too alarming. Whatever the case, human beings dream of the capability of greater expression.

Chapter 27: Lost

It is unfortunate to be lost on a highway; it is a terrible affliction to lose one's direction within the mind. Clouds can be beautiful in Earth's skies. However, clouds in one's consciousness are terrible sights. It is completely normal to lose one's way. It builds character.

How does one cure a cloudy mind? First, one may meditate on life's truths. There exist certain axioms that can aid in the awakening of greater consciousness. Next, one may be more mindful of one's surroundings, internally and externally. This should also help to clarify consciousness with an increased lucidity. Another possible solution is food and water. The absence of the body's needs is a simple problem to address; but, it is also an easy issue to overlook.

Moreover, I will here advise that if the cloudiness is severe enough, one should consult a professional. Losing mental direction could be a sign of sickness, physical and/or mental.

There is no shame in losing one's grasp on clarity. But, there is a wonderful pride that can be claimed in making an effort to improve once more.

Just because you're lost, doesn't mean you're lost. Adolf Hitler arguably had a good taste in the application of paint. If even a monster can see through the veil of greater love, then how much more can you, in your own sorrow, see through the darkness of the world, which has covered your mind with dark sheets. There is hope. Take that hope with you, so long as you are not yet another Hitler. If you are a Hitler, then please avoid my words. My pearls are best taken by queens, not swine.

Chapter 28: Gratitude

What is gratitude, if not the cornerstone of sanity? Ever moment holds a choice for our conscious minds to consider. A man who is four foot tall could be saddened by his shortness. Or, he could meditate on his height compared to a three foot tall fellow. Perspective, and the manipulation thereof, is the key to either the doorway towards our misery or to the place of our inner paradise.

Our minds are animals who need to be tamed by our own awareness. One must choose happiness, peace, and joy. One must also accept when those items are absent, whilst reminding the mind to be thankful regardless of immediate circumstances. The student of mindfulness needs to take control of the mind. For, the mind is often problematic when left to its own devices. Gratitude is a medicine which assists in the cure of true suffering. A woman may lose her husband, but she may be thankful that she was beautiful enough to have had the privilege of a fiery romance earlier in her life.

During my time in Ukraine, I witnessed a sight of which was alien to me. A man traveled on a board with wheels. This was no skateboard; the man riding the invention had no legs. I have felt the pain of a kidney stone, a broken heart, and the burn of a cigarette pressed into my hand; but, through it all – I have two legs.

Don't let your mind trick you. The concept that you are suffering the most is unlikely, and usually laughable. Free yourself from illusions. You are not suffering the most. You are not the center of the universe. You are not being punished by the world. Be grateful, and recognize the happiness, no matter how small, that you do possess. Notice that, whatever your situation, that your issues could be worse. Do not let the mind fool you. The mind can be a tool, but only when it is used properly. You may complain at the absence of an owner's manual. However, what do you believe this book to be? Meditate on these words.

Chapter 29: Play

I have the fondest memories of precious time shared with my cousins, with block toys, video games, and with my stuffed animals. To this day, I attempt to dedicate a portion of my daily meditations to that beloved pastime. The child plays in preparation for adulthood. The adult plays to relieve his woes.

Play is not a simple thing. It can be done alone, or with others. In the case of the latter, it is a social behavior. In the event of the former, it is a reflective action. Play is a way to express something true about the world, without the pressure of taking oneself all too seriously. There is a reason that acting performances are called plays. One does not need expensive toys; one merely needs an imagination to play.

Although they rarely admit to it, adults love to play. Adults never stop being children, just as apes never stopped being monkeys. And, play does not become something that is only some vestigial growth. It is necessary for the young girl and the grown woman alike. I wonder what games await us when we meet our Master once again.

Chapter 30: Dream

In the year of our Lord 2020, I had a rather fantastic dream. There was an Asian woman. She was fairly young, perhaps in her twenties, judging by her appearance. She taught me a new mudra. Oh, how I regret not drawing it! The positions of the hands now escape me. She told me to straighten my back as I sat. This is a common lesson in meditation, pranayama, etcetera.

Dreams are great mysteries among mysteries. Are they lessons? Do they hold the keys to prophesy and greater knowledge? Would they be more valuable if the dreamer were more aware? Why is time different for the dreamer than for the women of that other dream of the waking self? Are the people in the dream world conscious beings? Is the dream plane a working part of an objective reality?

I still wonder if someone, somewhere has cared enough to communicate with me in the dream world. Or, if it was all a fantasy of my imagination. Or, like life; perhaps it was all a little bit of both. Good night.

Chapter 31: Pain

There is a pressure in my shoulders, a muddiness in the streams of my spirit. It is a hard to define aspect of our nature. I feel my muscles tense. I possess the urge to release tears, but shed none. I desire to relieve my emotions through my strength, though rationality wins me over with flowers. I simultaneously appreciate it, and despise it vehemently. My heart has long been plagued with the phantom of pain. The pain that I reference here is not a physical pain, although it can manifest as such. It is a deeply rooted metaphorical tree of death. It steels my breath, and it crushes my hopes and dreams. I am assured that the greatest men of the world died horrifyingly terrible deaths. I am also left to wonder; what lies ahead?

Words can hurt. People hold such a wonderful gift; the gift of human language. Why, then, do so many individuals use it to keep folk up at night? It is cruel to curse a creature who is so beautiful. We should care what we say. Language is a woman who shines like a thousand Suns, even without makeup. Respect her. Love her. Be careful.

Chapter 32: Legalization

It's a bit taboo, this topic encircling the liberties, and lack thereof, of "illicit" substance use. Now, I personally don't encourage anyone to take any drug not prescribed by a competent doctor. Moreover, legalization doesn't mean "drugs are good". The subject is more complicated and delicate than some would have you believe.

First and foremost, the legalization of all drugs is the most powerful punch one can take against those giants who distribute, and gain power from, substances illegally. By keeping certain drugs illegal, we are also keeping certain dangerous people in power. There is a long history of the human (and non-human) use of psychoactive chemicals. The choice is not between drugs and no drugs, but between blood in the streets and peace. I strongly believe that legalizing drugs will ensure greater peace in our neighborhoods.

And, what of American liberty? What of pursuing happiness by one's own autonomy? The freedom to choose if one wants to try various drugs appears more American than baseball. Yet, such a fundamental human right is ignored by those in power. Take them out of power. Replace modern politicians with individuals who actually care about the founding principles of our great nation. Again, I am not encouraging drug use without the moderation of a good doctor; I am encouraging G-d's gift of free will to be permitted within the boarders of the United States. Without access to true freedom and liberty, America is disrespecting the lives of its soldiers who believe in freedom often to their dying breaths. Our troops deserve better, and so does every one of us.

Also, consider taxation. Think about the money that cigarettes and alcohol bring into local governments. Right now, all the money from illegal drugs is going into black market economies. Our schools and roads could benefit from large quantities of that capital. The argument that some people will still buy drugs illegally is ridiculous. Do you honestly believe that this isn't already happening with cigarettes and alcohol? The difference is that, since the majority of people follow the law (generally speaking) the government still benefits from the taxes of legal drugs like cigarettes.

Furthermore, legalizing drugs would help grow scientific research into the effects of various substances. Contemporarily, this is often difficult. It would help our entire society to know just how dangerous certain drugs are. Said research may even help prevent drug usage.

Finally, the legalization of all drugs would allow for a much heavier moderation of drugs used, as well as those who use them. Drug examinations could still be administered by employers. And, for those who take "illicit" drugs; one could sue the distributor if their "batch" were laced with something dangerous.

Chapter 33: La Perspectiva

La perspectiva es la arcilla de la vida. La moldeamos de acuerdo a nos deseos ocultos. La perspectiva es una elección, una preferencia de la mente. La perspectiva de la alma es una perla más preciosa. Es una cosa sagrada. En las cerámicas del cerebro, la perspectiva es un florero delicado.

¿Cuál es la perspectiva? Esta cosa es una habilidad o unas cadenas. La diferencia está en la cantidad de la conciencia. La perspectiva es una criatura que vive. Es la verdad metafóricamente que es un florero, pero tiene un corazón que late.

El cielo es azul solo para una persona, o alguno animal, que puede ve el color azul. A veces, el pelo de una mujer joven solamente tiene un buen olor para el hombre que tiene las memorias buenas sobre el pelo de las personas importantes para él. Tal vez, el sol es más caliente para la gata que la lagartija. Así, la perspectiva es plástica. La puede cambia, y es diferente dependiendo del contexto.

Chapter 34: Music

Music is a universal language, an antidote for the woes of the poor, a mandala of supreme meditation. It is the inspiration of the saints, the fuel of the jogger, the love of the heartbroken. The singer expresses what words alone lack, and the listener expands his soul to envelop the infinite within a black hole of desire. Music teaches us, good things and bad, what other social circles don't so much as whisper about.

The entire human race dances and sings, yet the observer judges some songs and dances as illegitimate. Perhaps mankind should be humbled, and take special note of the movements and melodical notes around it. If the woman knew she was dancing, then she may be freed of the chains of her sorrow. If the man only knew he was singing, he may escape his prison of suffering – if only for a moment! Do not the Gods enjoy dancing and singing? Don't we all have something of the Divine within us? There is godliness even in the lowly hominid. We've been dancing and singing since before we left the trees. Our close relatives, the chimpanzees, dance and sing to this day. We are animals. But, we are filled with potential. That potential shouldn't be overlooked. Why not dance and sing in the darkest hour of our night? We can always light a candle. Even a small candle burns bright in greater darkness. It is time to recognize the music that is all around us every day.

Chapter 35: The Poems

Saints of the World

Oh Muhammad! How many times did you beg for the faithful to pray?

Beloved Joseph Smith. How oft did you translate sin into righteousness?

My Savior. What hidden pains have you suffered for your brothers and sisters?

Oh Sathya Sai Baba. When have you manifested love from empty hate?

Mani! How many mighty men have been forgotten to time?

Oh Buddha Siddhartha. When do you meditate on the complexities of existence?

Sweet Nanak. What lessons of greater devotion do you possess for humanity?

My Lehi… Where may I find the concealed scriptures?

Adam, my father! How many creatures have you borne in your suffering?

Shiva of the East. When will you kill the pains of the Earth?

Bahá'u'láh; what tablets are yet to be revealed?

Oh loved ones of the planet; will my voice echo a reply?

Endless

The sky is endless.
The human without limit.
The world without start.

The Men

The smart man can think.
The wise man will meditate.
Both acts hold beauty.

Chapter 36: sdrawkcaB

semitemoS eth dlrow sleef sdrawkcab. erehT si a deviecrep ytinasni ot siht elbmuh ecnetsixe. ohW era eht stnias fo ruo tsomrenni serised? erehW era eht sdog fo ym s'luos tnaw? tahW era eht stneve taht lliw dlofnu nihtiw ruo tsriht rof hturt?

semitemoS eth dlrow sleef sdrawkcab. saH ti reve neeb yna rehto yaw? fI eht dlrow si, deedni, sdrawkcab; neht, tahw si sdrawrof? saH ton eht esrever emoceb eht emas sa sti etisoppo? rO, si ereht a ecnereffid, on rettam woh eltbus? ohW swonk? ohW swonk?

semitemoS eth dlrow sleef sdrawkcab. erehT si ecitsujni, dertah, raef, emirc, gnireffus, dna htaed. woH od ew evom drawrof? eW tsum pots eht drawkcab stnemele of our own lives.

Chapter 37: Facts

Facts are made of metal. Theories are synthesized from rubber. And, hypotheses are made of various plastics, from cheap and brittle - to string and durable.

There is a precedent for facts to change; nothing in science is sacred. At least, not in the sense that anything can be beyond criticism. Science is a harsh woman, punishing children who have not responded well to positive nor negative reinforcement. She gets results, even if the world doesn't always love her. It's not her fault that her children didn't respond to commonly successful methods; some people never seem to respond to the preferred methodologies.

We should all be aware that facts are not necessarily permanent. They are a way by which humans attempt to comprehend an incomprehensible universe. They are tools of our understanding. Humans like using tools. Let us not mistake facts for righteous and immortal gods. Let us think of them as individuals, like you and myself; prone to mistakes and imperfections.

<u>Chapter 38: La Poesía</u>

¿Algo Como Nada?

¿Cuál es la diferencia entre algo y nada?
Si nada puede manifestarse como un
pensamiento,
entonces ¿no es así también algo?

Luz Oscura

Si la luz borra la oscuridad, entonces
¿qué elimina el mundo de la luz?
O, contrariamente a la creencia popular,
¿la oscuridad quita la luz?

Dolor Gozoso

¿Es la alegría meramente la reacción del
cuerpo al dolor?
¿Pueden los dos separarse?
¿Es posible para el amor a existir sin el
odio?

Pluralismo Monoteísta

¿Hay algo que está ausente de las
dicotomías excepto por D--s?
Aún, ¿No los mazdanasios presentan,
su arquetipo del Todopoderoso como el Yin
a un Yang?

La Salvación es un Principio

La salvación de cualquier tipo no puede
existe como un medio para un fin.
Aquellos quienes lo buscan muy duro,
nunca paran en sus labores.

A Hablar

La comunicación es como un pájaro quien
está alto en el cielo.
Mucha gente en el suelo va a ver ella,
pero, nadie va a tocar sus plumas.

La Luz Divina

Vamos a rebobinar a nuestra discusión sobre
la luz.
La oscuridad solo puede ser contenido,
pero la luz es un dios quien puede ser
creado.

La Cura Para La Crueldad

La única cura para un mundo cruel es la
amabilidad.
Solo las lágrimas pueden quitar la ira.
La humildad ante la adversidad es una
virtud.

La maldad solo es alimentada por más
maldad.
La paz no siempre es la respuesta.
Tampoco es admitir la derrota.
A veces a luchar es bueno.
La única cura para un mundo cruel es la
amabilidad.
Se amable. Se paciente. No te rindas.
La cobardía es un vicio.

Extraño Mi Verdadero Amor

Extraño mi verdadero amor.
Quiero sentir tu corazón latir a través de tu
pecho.
Deseo el sabor de tus suaves labios.
Extraño el sonido de tu voz suave.
Recuerdo tus dedos de los pies y la parte
superior de tu cabeza.
Siempre me preocuparé por ti.
¿He encontrado mi verdadero amor dentro
de mi corazón?
¿Dónde nadie puede llevarse?
¿Dónde no se pierde realmente ninguna
posesión?
Busco a mi desposada fuera de mi
Pero, el interior se compara con el exterior.
¿Falta sabiduría?
Extraño a mi verdadero amor.

¿Cuántos, Ay Señor?

¿Cuántos, ay Señor?
¿Cuántos Manis se han caído duro por las edades?
¿Cuántos Abrahánes han roto los ídolos de la decepción?
¿Cuántos Haile Selassies han levantado nuestro hogar en unidad desde la multiplicidad?
¿Cuántos Moiséses han dividido los mares de la ignorancia?
¿Cuántos Zoroastros han predicado la luz en un mundo lleno con oscuridad?
¿Con qué frecuencia tiene la historia ha repetido sus propios evangelios y traumas? Tú que presides sobre los presidentes – por favor, muestra la misericordia a tus mensajeros.
¿Cuántos Davides han matado a los Goliates de la duda?
¿Cuántos Jonáses se han escapado de los peces de la pereza?
¿Cuántos Noé han navegado sobre el océano de la locura?
¿Cuántos Pablos han aprendido de la experiencia otorgada por la maravilla de la vida?

¿Cuántos Nefis han mantenido su fe en la adversidad?

¿Cuántos profetas han sido quemados, disparados, y crucificados?

Dios de todos los dioses – por favor, da paz y bendiciones a todos tus elegidos.

¿Cuántos José Smiths han traducido la arrogancia a humildad?

¿Cuántos Siddhartas han educado a los pobres?

¿Cuántos Juanes han bautizado con las aguas de redención?

¿Cuántos Mahomas han entregado libros de Dios?

¿Cuántos Adanes han realizado un acto de gran influencia?

¿Cuántos veces tiene la conciencia se ha crecido en conciencia dentro de las vastas aguas del tiempo?

Deidad de mujer y hombre – por favor, ayude a sus hijos a no perecer.

¿Cuántos Krishnas tocaron la música de la verdad a través de sus flautas de entendimiento?

¿Cuántos Salomones han pedido poco más que sabiduría?

¿Cuántos Isaíases han predicado la verdad a su pueblo?

¿Cuántos Akenatones han reverenciado a un
Dios por encima de los demás?
¿Cuántos Brigham Youngs han guiado a su
gente a una tierra elegida?
¿Cuántos seres han sufrido por el nombre de
su Deidad?
Ay Dios de los ángeles – por favor, ayuda a
todos tus sirvientes.

Ella Quien Tiene Ojos

El final está en al principio.
El principio está en el final.
Cada flor florece y muere.
Del suelo lo viene y lo va.
Ella quien tiene ojos, déjala ver.
Las estrellas brillan en cada ser.
Hay luces para el día y la noche.
Ninguna sombra puede igualar al sol.
Cada sombra proviene de la luz.
Ella quien tiene ojos, déjala leer.

No Soy

No soy mis pensamientos.
No soy mis emociones.
Yo veo.
No soy mi vientre, mis pies, o mis dedos.
Yo veo.
No soy mi pelo.

No soy mis manos.
Yo veo.
No soy mis palabras, acciones, o
actividades.
Yo veo.

En La Oscuridad De Mi Noche

En la oscuridad de la noche de mi corazón,
mi luz es más brillante.
Los cansados que se van a la cama,
duermen y están descansados mucho más.
La comida para la persona llena no es nada.
La riqueza para los ricos es redundante.
Este lado del velo parece necesitar,
un recordatorio de todas las cosas en
dualidad.

Ay Señor De La Montaña

Ay Señor de la montaña,
desciende hacia tus hijos.
¿Por qué no bajas?
¿Te estás escondiendo?
¿Estás más cerca de tu sol?
Ay Dios de todos los demás dioses,
Por favor baja de la montaña.
Tus hijos te aman.
Queremos verte en carne y hueso.
Eres el único Dios –

presidiendo sobre todos los presidentes,
Rey de reyes,
Maestro de maestros,
El mayor Amante entre los amantes.
Por favor mantén el perdón,
y por favor da la misericordia.
Eres el perdonador en medio de los
perdonadores,
el Misericordioso entre los misericordiosos.
Eres Señor de más que la montaña.

Chapter 39: Abuse

There is a seemingly endless abyss. It is a dark place, devoid of emotions. Yet, emotions are present. They're simply hidden from what little light enters the caverns of true misfortune.

Substance abuse is a serious problem for many individuals. Fortunately, many people (perhaps even the majority) grow out of this phase. For others, it is a cursed lifestyle. Addiction often begins with trauma. I still remember when my former girlfriend died. I remember when one of my friends died. Death after death, and I held it all in for years. One of the most concerning issues relating to sexism in our country, is the product of men who are preoccupied with the mission of hiding all negative emotions. The total repression of emotions is a concealed monster, waiting in the recesses of the collective psyche.

Substance abuse is not the answer to any problem. Trying to escape from one's emotions does no good. In fact, it may make the situation more problematic. For example, if a woman knows that a chemical can take her mind off of working to support her children, then she may very well choose her drug of choice over the wellbeing of her own kids.

Chapter 40: Feminism

Feminism, as defined as a movement searching for the equal rights of the genders, is good. Feminism, as thought of as a tool to hurt men, is bad. The men's rights activist movement was seemingly, at least in part, grown from concern for the latter conception. Discrimination is wrong, regardless of the sex or race. There is a point to be made that both genders face prejudice, even if women often take the worst of it.

I am a feminist. Our society is polluted with stereotypes and preconceived notions about what it means to be male and female. Members of each gender should feel as equals, not as separate entities. And, the revolution needs to be seeds planted into the hearts of individuals.

The prophet Muhammad, in his final sermon to the world, asked for women to be treated well. The poet Aleister Crowley once wrote that both women and men are, equally apparently, stars. The beloved Savior gave respect and love to the women in his life. Whether Muslim or Christian, Thelemite or Atheist; one should treat both genders with care, love, and fairness.

Chapter 41: "F" Is

"F" is for "final". This is the final chapter; of my book, but never of the endlessness of my entity. All things will change. Change only means an end for those who refuse to accept said change. Change is an opportunity; it is not necessarily death. Perhaps the concept of death is a human construct. But, then, what is life?

"F" is for "failure". It is that which leads to true success. Failure is a great teacher. The class isn't easy, but there is so much knowledge to be gained. How many times does a woman strike two rocks before gaining a single flame? How oft will a baby fall before he can proudly stand?

"F" is for "fate". He is an animal similar to beloved faith, but less forgiving. Fate is an outdated method for seeing the world. That is why "f" is also for "faith". Faith is the hope in the best the world has to offer. Faith is a bright star in the darkest of nights. Faith keeps the human being ticking in the best possible way. Faith is a lover who keeps his promises.

"F" is for "future". We all have one. It is the hope of the hopeless, the promise of the faithful, the growing concern of the comfortable. And, it is something that should sometimes be ignored. Not always, but sometimes. The present moment is often so important that we miss it. And, what is the future without more moments in the present?

"F" is for "finding". Life is simply filled with discovery. One finds many paths of life's journeys. Discovery is what keeps the heart of the soul satisfied with the continuity of existence. One longs to find. Finding implies loss. Whatever have we lost? Yet, we all are looking, searching.

"F" is for "fight". Even the good man must do battle. There are so many opportunities to fight; yet, we are burdened with the task of discovering when and where we actually should fight. It is a curious thing.

"F" is fabulously for a friendly yet finite number of fings. "F" is a fantastically fine letter. "F" is forever filed as it is.

"F" is for "fun". Go and have some. There is a whole world waiting for your presence, your inspiration, your love, and, even, your pain.